Colorado

WILD and BEAUTIFUL

PHOTOGRAPHY AND TEXT BY GLENN RANDALL

FARCOUNTRY
PRESS

TITLE PAGE: For residents and visitors alike, the Maroon Bells epitomize Colorado's beauty. The Bells, as they're known to locals, are made up of Maroon Peak (14,156 feet, left) and North Maroon Peak (14,014 feet). These aspen trees surrounding Maroon Lake were the most vibrant yellow I have ever seen.

RIGHT: The only waterfall I know of in Colorado that is lit by the sun at the moment of sunrise is Columbine Falls, along the Roaring Fork of Cabin Creek on the east flank of Longs Peak in Rocky Mountain National Park. I have photographed this falls nine times, in all seasons and from many angles. This photo and the cover are my two favorites.

FRONT COVER: On clear mornings, the intense orange and pink of the light from the rising sun is diluted by light from the bright, white sky surrounding the sun. The result is usually a pastel color, as if Nature had mixed white paint with red. On certain rare mornings, however, dense clouds block that bright, white light while the sun finds a tiny gap between the clouds and the horizon. The result is a pure, saturated beam of colorful light that here illuminates a cascade near Columbine Falls on the eastern flank of Longs Peak.

BACK COVER: In the Indian Peaks Wilderness near Grand Lake, sunset light floods into Wheeler Basin and bathes 13,150-foot Arikaree Peak while columbine bloom below in the lengthening evening shadows.

FRONT FLAP: The standing lenticular clouds over 14,255-foot Longs Peak are testimony to powerful winds aloft. The clouds are called "lenticular" because their cross-section is similar to that of a lens. They are said to be "standing" because the clouds themselves are stationary, while the wind blows through them. Evidence of powerful winds can also be seen in the *sastrugi*, or wind-carved snow, on the flanks of Flattop Mountain. In the winter, the wind on Longs Peak averages 65 mph–enough to knock a mountaineer to his knees. On one day in five, it averages 100 mph–enough to make it difficult to crawl.

ISBN 10: 1-56037-358-X
ISBN 13: 978-1-56037-358-2
Photography © 2005 by Glenn Randall
© 2005 Farcountry Press
Text by Glenn Randall

For more information about our books write Farcountry Press, P.O. Box 5630, Helena, MT 59604; call (800) 821-3874; or visit www.farcountrypress.com.

Created, produced, and designed in the United States.

INTRODUCTION

With a grunt, the baggage-handler on the Durango & Silverton Narrow Gauge Railroad wrestled my gigantic red pack out from the shadowy depths of the baggage car.

"There's the beast!" I said.

"That *is* a beast," a fellow backpacker behind me said, his voice tinged with admiration–or was it disdain and disbelief?

No matter: I had what I needed, and no more. Biceps straining, I hoisted my 70-pound load–about half my body weight–and started towards Chicago Basin, six miles away and 3,000 feet above me.

Half my load was large-format camera equipment. The other half was the food and gear essential for five days of wilderness landscape photography. Two-thirds of my solo journey through the Weminuche Wilderness would be off-trail. The crampons lashed to the pack would be essential for descending the steep snow on the north side of 13,080-foot Twin Thumbs Pass.

It was July 7, 2004. I had been planning this photo shoot for three years. Each year, drought and wildfires had stymied me at the last minute. Finally, in 2004, the drought eased, and my audacious plan became sweat-stained, arduous reality. At last I was going to explore, in-depth, one of the few mountain ranges in Colorado that I had never photographed.

I had first fallen in love with Colorado almost 30 years earlier, when I moved to Boulder to attend the University of Colorado and pursue my passion for adventure sports. In December, 1978, I graduated with a degree in journalism. With few skills and less money, but with an abundance of naïve optimism, I became a freelance writer and photographer. My beat was obvious: the outdoors.

I could not have found a better state to pursue my fledgling career. Colorado has 637 peaks that top 13,000 feet. Fifty-four scrape the sky at 14,000 feet or more. Coloradans call these "fourteeners." California has only 13 fourteeners; Washington state has but one, while Wyoming and Montana have none. Positioned near the southern end of the Rocky Mountains, which stretch from Alaska to New Mexico, Colorado's mountains receive abundant moisture from the summer monsoons that sweep across the desert Southwest. Winter snows pile up deep, filling the creeks and rivers with snowmelt come springtime. The Colorado Rockies are young enough to be rugged and picturesque, yet old enough to have developed the rich soils that support lush wildflower displays.

During the 1980s and into the early '90s, I saw the state through a climber's eyes. For my first book of photographs, *Vertigo Games*, I crisscrossed the mountains, photographing rock-climbers, ice-climbers, and mountaineers. To get the best shots, I frequently climbed the route myself, or else scrambled to the top via an easier route, then descended on a rope to position myself near the lead climber. I took up skiing and began adding ski-mountaineering photos to my

ABOVE: Parry primrose, a showy flower named for botanist Charles C. Parry, grows along Cunningham Creek in the Weminuche Wilderness near Silverton. The plant's skunky odor is so pungent that hikers often smell it before they see it.

FACING PAGE: Parry primrose grows profusely along the north fork of Middle Boulder Creek below Mount Neva, named by early prospectors for an Arapaho Indian.

collection. That effort culminated when I photographed Lou Dawson, the first person to ski all 54 fourteeners, make the second ski descent of the precipitous south face of Crestone Needle in the Sangre de Cristo Range.

In 1985, some friends invited me to go rafting on the Yampa River in Dinosaur National Monument, in Colorado's northwest corner. Suddenly I realized that the mountains that had dominated my explorations so far made up only two-fifths of the state. Dinosaur is certainly home to some of the most impressive dinosaur fossils ever unearthed, but it is also much more: a 329-square-mile expanse of 1,500-foot-deep, water-carved, sandstone canyons reminiscent of southern Utah. The five-day journey opened my eyes to an entirely new and dramatically different part of Colorado that I didn't know existed.

In 1989 I married, and my interest in extreme sports began to wane. My wife Cora is an endurance athlete, but not a climber. For our summer sport, we chose backpacking, and I began to see the state through new eyes. Instead of seeking out the steepest cliffs and tallest frozen waterfalls, I began searching for the most photogenic landscapes. I spent many hours studying topographic maps, looking for dramatic peaks that would receive spectacular light at sunrise or sunset. Once I found a promising location on the map, I visited it in person, seeking a special foreground–wildflowers, a waterfall, a wind-twisted snag–to make the image unique. Then I returned at sunrise or sunset, hoping to find the intersection of magical light and stunning subject matter that makes for an exceptional image. Most of the time, the images on film fell short of the images in my mind's eye. Although I can usually make at least one publishable photograph almost every day in the field, I find it takes me about 10 days, on average, to create one truly compelling image.

My 35mm camera equipment had served me well when photographing outdoor sports. However, it gave me inadequate detail when I began making big prints of my landscape images, so in 1993 I bought my first 4x5 field camera. These cameras use sheet film measuring 4x5 inches, which allows me to capture the smallest detail with startling clarity. Digital cameras are making rapid strides but still can't compete with the quality of large-format film.

I started my photographic exploration of Colorado's scenic beauty amidst the glacier-carved, granite peaks of Rocky Mountain National Park and the Indian Peaks Wilderness near my home in Boulder. Both ranges rise abruptly above the plains, which means that light from the rising sun travels an unusually long distance through the atmosphere before striking the summits. Geography and atmospheric optics bless both ranges with extraordinary sunrise light. In the past I had risen at 2 a.m. to climb a hard route on a high peak before the afternoon thunderstorms hit. Now I rose at 2 a.m. to photograph sunrise light striking those same vertical walls.

Next I fell in love with the Maroon Bells-Snowmass Wilderness, which lies between Aspen and Crested Butte. Here fertile soils and abundant moisture produce flowers in an abundance that astonished me after years of photographing the windswept tundra of the Front Range near Boulder. In the fall, some of the largest aspen groves in the state turn to shimmering gold beneath peaks frosted with the first snow.

After spending years backpacking into almost every major valley in the Maroon Bells-Snowmass Wilderness, I headed southwest, this time to the legendary San Juan Mountains near Durango, Silverton, and Telluride. My first visits were in the fall, to photograph the Sneffels Range, Wilson Peak, Owl Creek Pass, Red Mountain Pass, and Molas Divide. But I also knew that the San Juans were home to renowned fields of wildflowers. In July 2004, the time had finally come to step off the Durango & Silverton Narrow Gauge Railroad, collect my pack from the baggage car, and plunge into the Weminuche Wilderness.

For the next five days, I was reminded regularly that great landscape photography is 1 percent inspiration and 99 percent perspiration. The first day was heart-pounding labor as I plodded up the well-trodden trail to my camp in Chicago Basin. On the second day the trails got fainter, then vanished completely at 13,080-foot Twin Thumbs Pass. I looked north and gulped. This was the jumping-off place. The next maintained trail lay three and a half days away, beyond two more high, trackless passes and three deep valleys choked with willows, fallen logs, and roaring streams. Amazingly steep granite peaks rose in every direction. This was true wilderness, as wild and untouched as any place left in the Lower 48. When I finally reached the railroad again at Elk Park at the end of my journey, I had exposed every sheet of film I brought and wished I had more.

After another week of backpacking in other parts of the Weminuche Wilderness that summer, it was time to explore other corners of this vast state. I visited the 800-year-old cliff dwellings at Mesa Verde National Park and the sandstone canyons and spires at Colorado National Monument near Grand Junction. Then I headed east, to the vast shortgrass prairies that make up two-fifths of Colorado. In September I traveled to Pawnee National Grassland, the setting for James Michener's novel *Centennial*. Here the chalky cliffs of Pawnee Buttes rise above prairies that are home to an astonishing array of birds, including hawks, falcons, rare mountain plovers, and lark buntings, Colorado's state bird.

From Pawnee Buttes I went south to Colorado's other national prairie preserve, Comanche National Grassland. Here frontier history looms large. Bent's Old Fort National Historic Site, on the Arkansas River near the grassland, evokes vivid memories of the days when fur trappers plied their trade along the Santa Fe

Wilson Peak reflected in an unnamed pond on Wilson Mesa on a crystalline late September day. At 14,017 feet, the peak is not the highest of Colorado's fourteeners, but is one of the most picturesque. The peak is named for A. D. Wilson, a cartographer and surveyor with the Hayden Survey that mapped much of the San Juan Mountains in 1874.

ABOVE: Vestal Peak (13,864 feet, left) and Arrow Peak (13,803 feet), part of the Grenadier Range in the San Juans, are reflected in a Vestal Basin pond. Vestal is the highest peak in the Grenadiers. The clean, sweeping, quartzite north face, called Wham Ridge, attracts skilled mountaineers.

Trail. On the grassland itself, the endless hot, hardscrabble prairie, dotted with prickly pear and cholla, gradually gives way to the broad, shallow canyons of the Purgatoire River.

I've now spent nearly 30 years exploring this extraordinarily diverse state. The photographs in this book represent the best images from that odyssey. Yet I still haven't exhausted the photographic possibilities. I still get excited pouring over maps, pondering the possibilities of summer solstice sunrises and winter solstice sunsets. Many valleys and canyons still beg to be explored. Many peaks and passes still beckon. The best photographs, I find, are true to their subject and yet larger than their subject because they capture something universal. They both portray a singular moment in time and create a sense of timeless beauty. Ultimately my best photographs work by evoking in the viewer the sense of wonder I felt at the moment of exposure. Even after 30 years, I still find that sense of wonder in Colorado's wild places, and I'm still fascinated with trying to put that sense of wonder on film.

RIGHT: Sunrise light caresses the soft contours of Peak 12,505 in the Maroon Bells-Snowmass Wilderness, near Aspen.

9

RIGHT: One of the great delights of the Maroon Bells-Snowmass Wilderness is how astonishingly green it is, like an alpine version of Ireland. Here alpine sunflowers grow in profusion near Hasley Pass overlooking Hasley Basin. On the skyline, Snowmass Mountain (14,092 feet) pokes up behind Hagerman Peak (13,841 feet) and Snowmass Peak (13,620 feet).

BELOW: A bull elk in velvet on Trail Ridge near Timberline Pass in Rocky Mountain National Park. The square-topped bulk of Longs Peak, the park's highest peak at 14,255 feet, is the leftmost peak on the skyline.

ABOVE: A hang-glider pilot launches from 12,736-foot Gold Hill, near Telluride, with the Sneffels Range in the background.

LEFT: Steamboat Springs was named after a spring along the Yampa River that gurgled and whistled like a steamboat laboring upstream. Mount Werner, its world-class ski runs awaiting its winter blanket of snow, rises in the background. The post-sunset glow to the west has turned the leaves of the gambel oaks in the foreground a fiery red.

RIGHT: The incline railway at Royal Gorge Bridge and Park, completed in 1931, shuttles tourists down precipitous Telephone Gulch to the banks of the Arkansas River and back. Royal Gorge is over 1,000 feet deep at its deepest point.

FACING PAGE: White petals of columbine in Pearl Basin glow pink when backlit by the rising sun, White River National Forest, near Aspen.

BELOW: The dunes at Great Sand Dunes National Park are the highest in North America. They tower 750 feet above the plains of the San Luis Valley near Alamosa. In the background rise 13,414-foot Cleveland Peak (left) and 13,297-foot Mount Herard of the Sangre de Cristo Range.

LEFT: A weathered juniper in Colorado National Monument near Grand Junction flushes pink in the dawn. The 450-foot sandstone monolith called Independence Monument rises in the top right. John Otto, an eccentric preservationist, engineered his way up the spire and planted an American flag on top as part of his campaign to preserve and promote the region, which became a national monument in 1911.

BELOW: Wind-sculpted snow, called *sastrugi* from a Russian word that means wind-carved furrow, glows at sunset below 13,365-foot Gold Dust Peak, Holy Cross Wilderness, near Vail.

RIGHT: Dense storm clouds wreathe Whitehouse Mountain in the Mount Sneffels Wilderness near Ridgway, while the setting sun bursts through the clouds at the western horizon and illuminates the aspen.

BELOW: Sunset light shines through perfect aspen leaves and makes them glow like stained glass in this view from Owl Creek Pass near Ridgway.

LEFT: Coyote Village, part of the Far View Sites at Mesa Verde National Park, was built and modified over the years from A.D. 900 to A.D. 1300. Located at 7,700 feet, it was high enough to attract adequate rainfall for growing corn, squash, and beans and low enough for a reasonable growing season between frosts.

BELOW: Charles and William Bent and their business partner Ceran St. Vrain built Bent's Old Fort in 1833 as a trading post along the Santa Fe Trail that extended west from Independence, Missouri, to Santa Fe, New Mexico. These wooden barrels at the fort were used to store a variety of goods, such as molasses, syrup, flour, sugar or salt.

RIGHT: A weather-beaten juniper frames South Gateway Rock in the Garden of the Gods, near Colorado Springs. Charles Elliot Perkins, an Iowa railroad builder, bought 240 acres of the Garden of the Gods in 1879, and later bought another 240 acres. After his death, his children gave the land to Colorado Springs to be a park open to the public, free of charge, forever.

BELOW: Warm sunset light accentuates the colors of these aspen groves on Buffalo Pass, near Steamboat Springs. Most aspen groves grow in deep valleys and are shadowed at the moment of sunset. To the west of Buffalo Pass, however, is the rolling basin and plateau country of Colorado's Western Slope, so there are no high peaks to block the sunset light.

ABOVE: The setting sun backlights tree cholla on the shortgrass prairie of Comanche National Grassland, in southeast Colorado, south of La Junta. Forbidding landscapes like this were a familiar sight to travelers on the nearby Santa Fe Trail.

FACING PAGE: The sun rises over Pawnee Buttes, Pawnee National Grassland, near Briggsdale. For more than 150 years, these crumbling towers have guided pioneers across the northeast Colorado plains. In the late 1800s and early 1900s, many homesteaders founded dry-land farms nearby. Starting in the 1920s, drought, poor farming practices, and low wheat prices made farming a struggle, and the infamous Dust Bowl of the 1930s finished off most of the farms.

LEFT: Canyon Doors, the first rapid in Gore Canyon on the Colorado River near Kremmling, is the opening challenge in one of Colorado's most difficult stretches of whitewater. When the river is high, as it was here, Gore Canyon can test the most experienced raft crew.

RIGHT: Millions of American bison (improperly called buffalo) once roamed the high plains and mountains of North America. Wanton slaughter by white settlers in the late 1800s reduced their numbers to near-extinction. This survivor rests comfortably in a pasture on Lookout Mountain west of Denver.

BELOW: Beavers, such as this one along the Green River in Dinosaur National Monument, were once prized for their pelts. Now some ranchers find them valuable for their ability to restore riparian areas damaged by overgrazing.

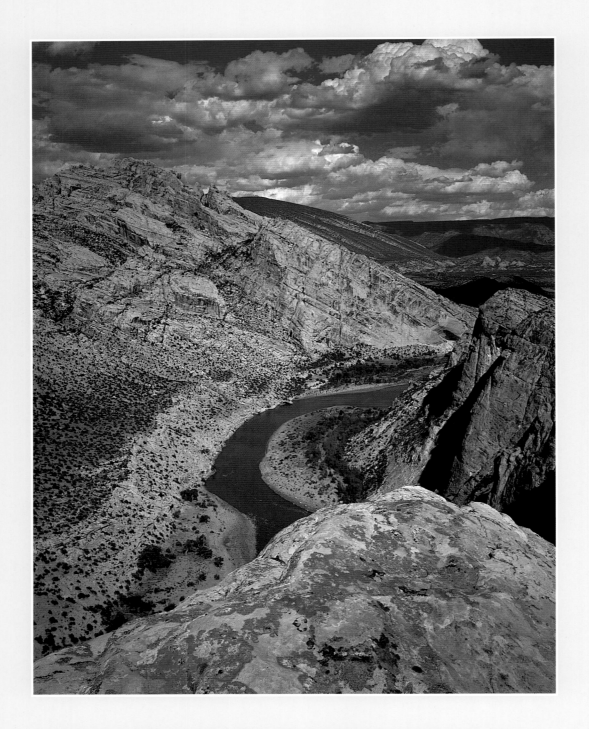

ABOVE: The Green River emerges from Split Mountain Canyon in Dinosaur National Monument. John Wesley Powell, a one-armed Civil War veteran, led the first expedition to explore the complete length of the Green and Colorado rivers in 1869.

RIGHT: The Dolores Mission, built in 1898, lies in ruins in Purgatoire Canyon, Comanche National Grassland, near La Junta.

LEFT: Many state wildlife areas dot the plains of eastern Colorado. Here clouds ignited by the setting sun float over Rocky Ford State Wildlife Area along the Arkansas River.

BELOW: The Green River flows through Split Mountain Canyon in this view from Ruple Point in Dinosaur National Monument. The monument straddles the Colorado/Utah line; this portion lies in Utah.

LEFT: The wind carved a graceful miniature cornice on the snow below the 13,521-foot Star Peak in the White River National Forest near Aspen. Within hours, wind from another direction filled it back in again.

BELOW: Small but formidable, 11,920-foot Lone Eagle Peak is hidden from every roadside vantage point. To see it reflected in Mirror Lake required a 16-mile round-trip hike through the Indian Peaks Wilderness near Grand Lake.

34

The aspen groves along the northern flank of the Sneffels Range near Ridgway are
leaf-peepers and shutterbugs. From left to right, the major peaks in this view are 13,
Mountain, 13,468-foot Mount Ridgway, Peak 12,960, 13,686-foot Cirque Mountain, a
east ridge of Mount Sneffels.

...ust-see for autumn
...-foot Whitehouse
... a tower along the

LEFT: I waited out four hours of rain, hail, and snow and was rewarded with the sight of 14,014-foot North Maroon Peak emerging from the clouds and casting its reflection on Maroon Lake in the Maroon Bells-Snowmass Wilderness near Aspen.

BELOW: Although only 11,348 feet, Marcellina Mountain looks bigger than it is when framed by aspen and covered with fog and fresh snow. Marcellina Mountain is one of several small but beautiful peaks that rise near Kebler Pass, site of some of the state's largest aspen groves.

ABOVE: Lichen on a ridge high above Buckskin Pass explodes with color when illuminated by the orange light of the rising sun. Two of the seven fourteeners found in the Maroon Bells-Snowmass Wilderness–14,092-foot Snowmass Mountain (left), and 14,130-foot Capitol Peak–rise in the background.

FACING PAGE: For one week each summer, the sun rises directly over the Lake Isabelle outlet in the Indian Peaks Wilderness near Boulder. The rocky stream in the foreground flows directly toward the rising sun. The sun's reflection has traced a pattern of gold lace on the rippled surface of the water.

ABOVE: A rainbow soars over an aspen grove on Dallas Divide, near Ridgway.

RIGHT: A brief clearing between autumn storms allows 13,496-foot Mears Peak and Peak 13,134 of the Sneffels Range to emerge from the clouds in this view from Dallas Divide, near Ridgway.

RIGHT: These mule deer fawns made themselves at home right below the back deck of my home in Boulder. They may well have been born in the dense brush in my backyard.

LEFT: Serviceberry blooms along the south rim of the Black Canyon of the Gunnison. Across the canyon is the Painted Wall, the highest cliff along the Gunnison River's awesome gorge, which plunges 2,250 feet from rim to river.

BELOW: Two mule deer bucks spar along a suburban side street in Boulder. The large mule-deer herds that live in the nearby Boulder Mountain Parks frequently descend into the city in winter, looking for easier forage.

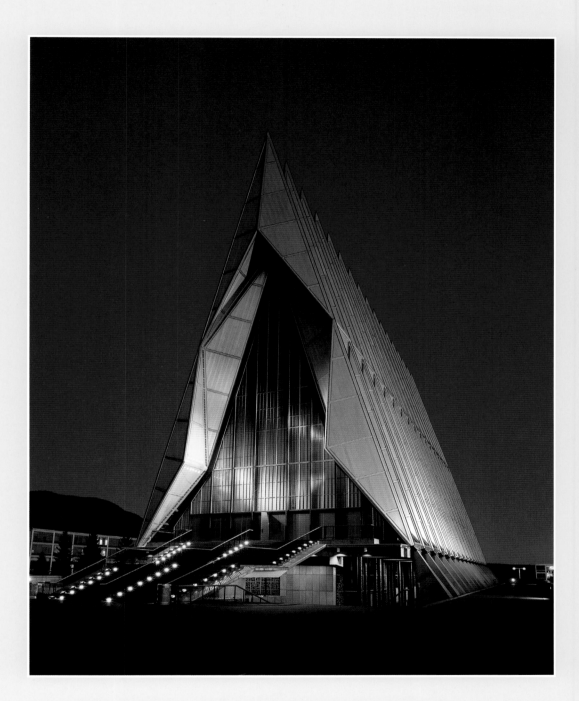

ABOVE: The interdenominational Cadet Chapel at the United States Air Force Academy, near Colorado Springs, was completed in 1963 after nine years of planning and construction.

LEFT: The downtown Denver skyline glows pink and orange in this sunrise photo from the Denver Museum of Nature and Science. Denver is Colorado's capital and its largest metropolitan area.

LEFT: The basin ringed by Hasley, Frigid Air, and West Maroon passes in the Maroon Bells-Snowmass Wilderness near Crested Butte is the most lush wildflower area I've photographed. "West Maroon Basin," as I call it, must also be one of the most well-watered valleys in Colorado. I photographed this field of lupine below unnamed 12,000-foot, green peaks in between driving rainstorms.

BELOW: Columbine grow everywhere in West Maroon Basin.

RIGHT: The aspen-clad flanks of Mount Owen (13,058 feet) and Ruby Peak (12,644 feet) in the Kebler Pass area near Crested Butte dominate this view from a remote granite knoll, which I located after a long, off-trail search.

BELOW: The highway over Red Mountain Pass between Ouray and Silverton is crooked enough to break a snake's back. In September, at the height of fall color, it makes for a glorious drive. In winter, massive avalanches frequently close the road.

ABOVE: Window Rock, Purgatoire Canyon, Comanche National Grassland, near La Junta. Locals use the English pronunciation and call the Purgatoire River the Purgatory. Early cowboys, who couldn't wrap their tongues around the French pronunciation of this sharply incised network of branching valleys, called the area the Picketwire Canyonlands. Whatever you call it, this 300-foot deep canyon is an anomaly on the relentlessly flat plains of eastern Colorado.

LEFT: Eroded gullies incise the shortgrass prairie of Pawnee National Grassland near Briggsdale. The grassland lies in the rain shadow of the Rockies and receives only 12 to 15 inches of precipitation per year, mostly as rain from April through June. Frequent high winds soon evaporate much of what little rain does fall.

RIGHT: South Colony Creek and 14,197-foot Crestone Needle, Sangre de Cristo Wilderness, near Westcliffe. One of Colorado's newest wildernesses, the Sangre de Cristo Wilderness was designated in 1993. Seventeenth-century Spanish missionaries and explorers gave the range its name, which means "blood of Christ," possibly because the peaks, which jut 7,000 feet above the valley floor, receive spectacular sunrise and sunset light.

FACING PAGE: Tired from a long drive the night before, I slept through both of my alarms, woke up late, and arrived at Maroon Lake barely in time to capture the midsummer sunrise light striking the 14,000-foot Maroon Bells. The delicate, lacy flower in the foreground goes by the inelegant name "cow parsnip." Although spectacular to look at, the Bells have earned the nickname "The Deadly Bells" for their rotten rock, which has killed a number of mountaineers attempting to scale their crumbling flanks.

LEFT: The light at sunset makes every ripple of Star Dune, the second-highest dune in Great Sand Dunes National Park, stand out in bold relief. The dominant peak on the right is 13,414-foot Mount Cleveland; beyond it in the distance to the left rise three fourteeners of the Sangre de Cristo Range: Kit Carson, Crestone Peak, and Crestone Needle.

BELOW: A bighorn ram near Cow Creek in Rocky Mountain National Park cautiously eyes the photographer. In the mid-1800s, thousands of bighorn sheep roamed the foothills and high peaks of Rocky Mountain National Park. By the 1950s, hunting, disease, and loss of habitat reduced their number to only 150. Today, aided by reintroduction efforts and reduced hunting and disease, the population has climbed to about 600.

RIGHT: At the entrance to the Narrows, the Black Canyon of the Gunnison is 1,600 feet deep. It took the Gunnison River two million years to cut its gorge through the two-billion-year-old gneiss and schist of the Black Canyon, a rate of only one inch every 100 years.

FACING PAGE: Columbine bloom along the trail to Arapaho Pass in the Indian Peaks Wilderness near Boulder. From left to right, the mountains are Peak 12,923, known locally as Jasper Peak; Peak 12,068; and Mount Neva at 12,814 feet.

LEFT: South Park City, in Fairplay, is an accurate reconstruction of a typical Colorado gold mining camp during the period from 1860 to 1900. Seven buildings are on their original sites. Others were moved from nearby mining camps in the 900-square-mile South Park mining district.

BELOW: White-tailed ptarmigan in summer plumage search for food below Pawnee Pass, Indian Peaks Wilderness, near Boulder. These hardy birds thrive in the alpine zone. They turn completely white in winter except for their black beaks and eyes. White feathers provide winter camouflage, of course, but also insulation. White feathers contain heat-trapping hollows, whereas colored feathers are filled with pigment.

RIGHT: The historic Crystal Mill (also called the Lost Horse Mill or Dead Horse Mill) was built in 1892 along the Crystal River, near Marble. By some accounts, the building once had a waterwheel that drove an air compressor, which powered drills at nearby mines.

BELOW: A yellowbelly marmot suns itself on the Continental Divide near Mount Ida in Rocky Mountain National Park. Marmots are one of the few animals that spend the winter in the high alpine zone. They hibernate from August to March.

LEFT: Towering thunderheads dwarf the 14,000-foot Maroon Bells in this view from West Maroon Basin in the Maroon Bells-Snowmass Wilderness, near Crested Butte. Lupine and two species of Indian paintbrush bloom in the foreground.

BELOW: Columbine, paintbrush, Rydberg's arnica, and lupine thrive in West Maroon Basin, Maroon Bells-Snowmass Wilderness, near Crested Butte.

Although I have photographed
the 14,000-foot Maroon Bells from
Maroon Lake at least a dozen times,
this sunrise view of the Bells in late
September is one of my favorites.

ABOVE: Partially excavated fossils of dinosaur bones protrude from the rock in the Douglass Dinosaur Quarry, Dinosaur National Monument. Discovered in 1909 by paleontologist Earl Douglass, these fossils are about 150 million years old. About 1,500 bones from 11 different kinds of dinosaurs can be seen at the quarry.

LEFT: Steamboat Rock soars out of a horseshoe bend in the Green River called Echo Park. Echo Park is one of the few places in Dinosaur National Monument where a road reaches the river.

ABOVE: Jack Roberts climbs a thin pillar of ice at Grace Falls in Rocky Mountain National Park.

RIGHT: Hallett Peak (12,713 feet) is reflected in Dream Lake during a winter sunrise in Rocky Mountain National Park. Hallett Peak was named for pioneer rancher, mining engineer, and mountaineer William Hallett.

BELOW: Jack Roberts climbs the Little Thang, a ferocious ice-climb near Vail. In winter, many seeps and small waterfalls freeze solid, allowing ice-climbers with sharp ice axes, ice hammers, and crampons to practice their daring, slippery sport.

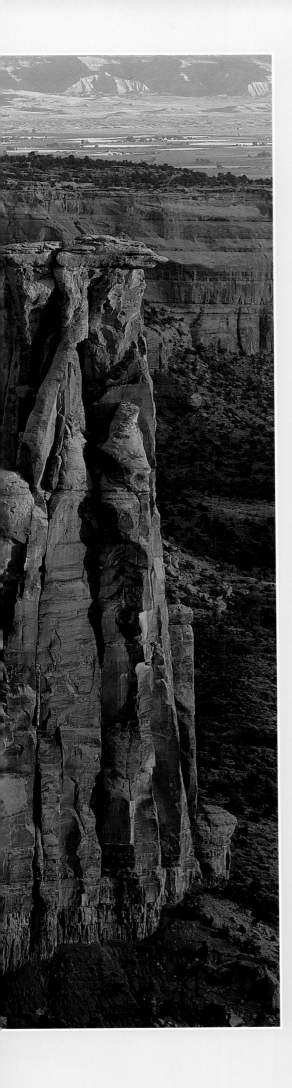

LEFT: Early light bathes the cliffs and spires of Colorado National Monument, near Grand Junction. On the right, in the foreground, is the Kissing Couple; behind and just to the left is Independence Monument. The spire in the far distance is the Pipe Organ.

BELOW: Whirlpool Canyon meanders toward the setting sun in this view from Harpers Corner in Dinosaur National Monument. John Wesley Powell named Whirlpool Canyon during his epic descent of the Green and Colorado rivers in 1869.

RIGHT: Although I have photographed the Maroon Bells several times in summer, only once have I seen fireweed blooming in such profusion along the shores of Maroon Lake near Aspen.

BELOW: A bighorn ram along Jones Hole Creek in Dinosaur National Monument pauses to inspect the intruder. The large, spring-fed creek has created a startling green oasis in an arid land.

LEFT: Sunset light floods the valley of Noname Creek and illuminates Peak 10 (13,400 feet, left) and Knife Point (13,265 feet) in the Weminuche Wilderness, near Durango. These jagged peaks are part of the Needle Mountains, a sub-range of the San Juans. I photographed them on the second day of the five-day backpacking adventure I described in the introduction. A field of skunk cabbage fills the foreground.

BELOW: Roseroot and skunk cabbage in Cumberland Basin in the La Plata Mountains near Durango.

RIGHT: Cliff Palace is the largest ancestral Puebloan structure in Mesa Verde National Park. (The ancestral Puebloan people were formerly called the Anasazi.) Construction began around A.D. 1200; by A.D. 1300 A.D., it had been abandoned. In 1978, the United Nations designated Mesa Verde as one of the first seven World Cultural Heritage Sites.

BELOW: Scarcely a breath of wind stirred on the late-September day when I photographed Longs Peak and Glacier Gorge from Bear Lake in Rocky Mountain National Park.

ABOVE: Lou Dawson powers through a jump turn in mashed-potato snow during the second known ski descent of the south face of 14,197-foot Crestone Needle in the Sangre de Cristo Wilderness near Westcliffe. In 1991, Dawson became the first person to ski all 54 of Colorado's 14,000-foot peaks.

LEFT: The famed Maroon Bells, 10 miles south of Aspen, draw some 200,000 visitors each summer and fall. In winter, however, the road is closed by snow. In March 2003, I hauled 100 pounds of large-format camera equipment and winter camping gear six miles up the snow-covered road and camped for three nights on the edge of Maroon Lake without seeing a soul.

LEFT: The only Colorado tree that turns red in the fall is the gambel oak, which grows in dense, shrubby thickets at moderate elevations. The peaks from left to right are Peak 13,072; Whitehouse Mountain (13,492 feet); Mount Ridgway (13,468 feet); Peak 12,960; Cirque Mountain (13,686 feet); and Mount Sneffels (14,150 feet). All are part of the Sneffels Range near Ridgway.

BELOW: Cora and Glenn Randall look over the valley of Lost Creek in the Lost Creek Wilderness near Bailey. Lost Creek got its name because it appears and disappears repeatedly as it winds through the aspen groves, granite domes, and complex valleys that make up this wilderness. The beautiful Lost Creek Wilderness is close to Denver, yet it lacks the high peaks that would draw visitors in large numbers.

RIGHT: Bill Miller chases Jennifer Fabian down the Outback at Keystone Ski Resort. To make this photograph, I mounted a camera and fisheye lens with a 180-degree angle of view on Miller's chest, then triggered the camera with a radio release as he skied by.

LEFT: Bill Miller catches air on The Plunge at Loveland Ski Area. Alpine skiers rack up 11.5 million skier visits each year in Colorado, more than California and Utah combined.

BELOW: Larry Coats cranks a turn on Taylor Glacier in Rocky Mountain National Park. Although nowhere near as numerous as alpine skiers, dedicated backcountry skiers in Colorado penetrate deep into the wilderness, particularly in the spring when the snowpack stabilizes and the avalanche danger diminishes.

LEFT: Dense clouds shrouded the peaks when I awoke at my camp at remote Balsam Lake in the Weminuche Wilderness near Durango. By the time I broke camp and began climbing toward the pass between Vestal and West Trinity peaks, however, the clouds had broken up, and I shot this photo looking south toward Peak 6 (13,705 feet) and Balsam Lake.

BELOW: This mountain goat kid in Chicago Basin in the Weminuche Wilderness near Durango had almost no fear of humans. Mountain goats are agile creatures who live at or above timberline in summer, then descend into the forest in winter. They can live to be 12 years old in the wild.

RIGHT: Sunset's golden light accentuates the color of these rare red aspen and gilds the multiple summits of 12,432-foot East Beckwith in the Kebler Pass area near Crested Butte. Most aspen in Colorado turn yellow in the fall. A few, however, turn orange or even red, depending on the concentrations of anthocyanins, the red pigments, and carotenoids, the yellow pigments. A succession of warm, clear days and cool, but not freezing, nights spurs the production of anthocyanins. These aspen at the base of Marcellina Mountain were among the reddest I had ever seen.

BELOW: Indian paintbrush below King Lake in the Indian Peaks Wilderness near Boulder glows when backlit by the rising sun. Indian paintbrush is one of the most common flowers in the Colorado Rockies.

ABOVE: Randy Leavitt contemplates the crux of Amazing Grace, a difficult rock climb in the Garden of the Gods, near Colorado Springs. The soft sandstone layers of the Lyons Formation, which makes up the Garden, were originally horizontal. An epoch of mountain-building 65 million years ago tilted them vertically and created a playground for rock-climbers as well as a delight for sightseers.

RIGHT: The weathered remains of a limber pine on Twin Sisters frames Longs Peak and Mount Meeker in Rocky Mountain National Park. Limber pines can live up to 700 years, but eventually even they succumb to the harsh timberline climate.

LEFT: Columbine bloom on a bench above Ruby Basin in the Weminuche Wilderness near Durango. The basin is ringed by 13,000-foot peaks, including 13,786-foot Animas Mountain. No maintained trail leads into Ruby Basin, which is visited only by ardent mountaineers, die-hard backpackers, and incurably obsessed photographers.

RIGHT: Long House, on Wetherill Mesa in Mesa Verde National Park, is the park's second-largest cliff dwelling. Construction began around A.D. 1200 Pots of pollen similar to those used in modern Pueblo ceremonies were found at the site, leading some archaeologists to speculate that Long House was built for ceremonial purposes, perhaps in an effort to reverse a long drought.

BELOW: These thousand-year-old pictographs were drawn by Fremont Indians in Jones Hole in Dinosaur National Monument.

ABOVE: The Needle Mountains catch the sunset light in this view from Peak 12,458 in the Weminuche Wilderness near Durango. It took me two days to reach this vantage point on the ridge overlooking the Animas River canyon. The sunlit peak in the center is 14,083-foot Mount Eolus. The farthest peak on the right is the 13,972-foot Pigeon Peak. On the left, Animas Mountain, Peak 13, and Monitor Peak are all thirteen-thousand-footers.

LEFT: I found this delicate group of columbine growing from a desolate and unstable scree field in Vestal Basin, in the Weminuche Wilderness near Durango.

RIGHT: Sunset-reddened cumulus clouds float over Forest Canyon in Rocky Mountain National Park. Longs Peak, (14,255 feet) looms at the far left. The skyline is part of the Continental Divide.

BELOW: Dinosaur Mountain forms the southern end of the Flatirons in this view from Bear Canyon in the Boulder Mountain Parks, near Boulder. The Flatirons are part of the Fountain Formation, a type of sandstone laid down about 280 million years ago. The Flatirons were tilted to their present angle by a mountain-building episode that began 65 million years ago.

LEFT: Storm clouds gather over the 10 Mile Range, near Breckenridge, while a shaft of sunlight illuminates a field of yellow mule's ears growing near Boreas Pass Road.

BELOW: Golden aspen line the Dunton Road in the San Juan Mountains near Rico.

RIGHT: Graceful, wind-sculpted pillows of snow contrast sharply with the jagged Maroon Bells in this view from Maroon Lake in the Maroon Bells-Snowmass Wilderness near Aspen. This part of Colorado was one of only five Colorado wildernesses designated in the original 1964 Wilderness Act.

BELOW: A bristlecone pine grows almost horizontally on Windy Ridge, near Alma. By bristlecone standards, the trees in the Windy Ridge Bristlecone Pine Scenic Area are babies–only 800 to 1,000 years old. They grow at about 11,700 feet and are warped into odd forms by the nearly constant wind that sweeps down the eastern flanks of 14,172-foot Mount Bross.

LEFT: On exceptionally clear days, particularly at high altitudes, a band of pink light called the twilight wedge forms in the sky to the west about 15 minutes before the sun crests the eastern horizon. This band is created by selective sorting of the different wavelengths of light during the light's long path through the atmosphere from east to west, then back to the viewer's eye after bouncing off air molecules and dust. During its lengthy journey, blue light scatters out of the beam, leaving behind only pink light to return to the viewer's eye. The band of blue beneath the band of pink is essentially the Earth's shadow. This twilight wedge has formed over the Yampa Valley as seen from Buffalo Pass, near Steamboat Springs.

BELOW: Royal Gorge Bridge was built over the Arkansas River in 1929 strictly to attract tourists. The main span stretches 880 feet. It stands 1,053 feet above the river, making the Royal Gorge Bridge the world's highest suspension bridge.

RIGHT: The east face of Longs Peak looms over Chasm Lake in Rocky Mountain National Park. Only foothills lie between 14,255-foot Longs Peak and the plains 9,000 feet below, so sunrise light floods unobstructed into one of the most spectacular alpine cirques in Colorado.

FACING PAGE: Sunrise light kisses the top of Vestal Peak (13,864 feet, left) and Arrow Peak (13,803 feet) in the Grenadier Range of the Weminuche Wilderness, near Durango. At nearly 500,000 acres, the Weminuche is twice the size of Colorado's next largest wilderness area.

LEFT: Chimney Rock (11,781 feet, left) and Courthouse Mountain (12,152 feet) catch the sunset light in late September. Owl Creek Pass, 10 miles east of Ridgway, is at the extreme left side of the picture.

BELOW: Sunset light turns yellow aspen to gold while the moon rides high over the Uncompahgre National Forest, near Telluride.

LEFT: Parry primrose and marsh marigolds bloom beneath Mount Neva (12,814 feet) in the Indian Peaks Wilderness, near Boulder. Despite the area's obvious wilderness qualities, it took 14 years after the signing of the 1964 Wilderness Act before the Indian Peaks received formal wilderness designation.

BELOW: Golden pea in the Maroon Bells-Snowmass Wilderness, near Aspen.

RIGHT: Early morning light accentuates the contours of the sand dunes beneath 13,414-foot Mount Cleveland in Great Sand Dunes National Park. The sand dunes were preserved as a national monument in 1932. The monument was expanded and became a national park in 2004.

BELOW: The moon floats over the capitol in Denver.

LEFT: The lack of a trail to remote Little Rock Lake in Rocky Mountain National Park guarantees solitude.

BELOW: This ancient limber pine near Lake Haiyaha in Rocky Mountain National Park may well have been growing there when Columbus arrived in America.

RIGHT: The last rays of the setting sun highlight Pawnee Buttes on the Pawnee National Grassland near Briggsdale, while the plains below are plunged into shadow. Pawnee Buttes and the nearby Chalk Bluffs are either home or a seasonal stopover for many raptors, including golden eagles, Swainson's hawks, red-tailed hawks, ferruginous hawks, and prairie falcons.

BELOW: Bent's Old Fort, on the Arkansas River near La Junta, was built in 1833 to serve traders along the Santa Fe Trail. At first, beaver pelts were a prized commodity; later, buffalo pelts became a staple trade good. The fort is now a National Historic Site.

LEFT: Indian paintbrush near Caribou Lake blooms profusely while an evening thunderstorm slowly clears, revealing Navaho Peak in the Indian Peaks Wilderness, near Boulder. In the Colorado Rockies, July is peak wildflower season. Not coincidentally, July also brings the onset of the "summer monsoon," with frequent rain showers and thunderstorms.

BELOW: Purple saxifrage grows along Icy Brook in Rocky Mountain National Park.

ABOVE: Cora Randall runs up the Flattop Trail in Rocky Mountain National Park. Hallett Peak (12,713 feet) rises behind. According to Northern Arapaho elders that historians consulted in 1914, Arapaho Indians once used this route over the Continental Divide, calling it the Big Trail.

FACING PAGE: Indian paintbrush and the Nokhu Crags at sunrise in the Never Summer Mountains, near Grand Lake.

ABOVE: Sunrise illuminates the rock formation called the Siamese Twins and 14,110-foot Pikes Peak in the Garden of the Gods near Colorado Springs.

LEFT: In late afternoon during a stormy September fall-color shoot in the San Juan Mountains, the sun found two holes in the clouds and separately spotlighted Peak 12,734 and a grove of unusual orange aspen growing near Silver Jack Reservoir.

FOLLOWING PAGE: Columbine, heartleaf arnica, and Indian paintbrush flower beneath Mount Toll in the Indian Peaks Wilderness near Boulder. The peak's name commemorates Roger Toll, superintendent of Rocky Mountain National Park from 1921 to 1929. Toll was instrumental in adding the Never Summer Mountains to Rocky Mountain National Park, but he failed in his efforts to add the Indian Peaks.